Living the
Consecrated Life
in the Third Millennium

A resource book for individuals and communities

Ronald J. McAinsh C.Ss.R.

Published by Redemptorist Publications

Alphonsus House
Chawton
Hampshire
GU34 3HQ
UK

Tel. +44 (0)1420 88222
Fax. +44 (0)1420 88805
Email rp@rpbooks.co.uk
www.rpbooks.co.uk

A registered charity limited by guarantee
Registered in England 3261721

Copyright © Redemptorist Publications 2014
First published November 2014

Designed by Nuttifox
Picture editor: Denis McBride C.Ss.R.

ISBN 978-0-85231-419-7

A CIP catalogue record for this book is available from the British Library.

Nihil Obstat: Rev. William Wilson, *Censor deputatis*
Imprimatur: + Rt. Rev. Philip A. Egan BA, STL, PhD
Bishop of Portsmouth
29th September 2014
The *Nihil Obstat* and *Imprimatur* are official declarations that a book or pamplet is free of doctrinal or moral error. No implication is contained therein that those who have granted the *Nihil Obstat* and *Imprimatur* agree with the contents, opinions or statements expressed.

Printed and bound by John Dollin Printing Services Limited,
Whitchurch, Hampshire

Ronald McAinsh is a Redemptorist who is currently provincial superior of the UK Province; he previously served as regional superior of the Redemptorists in Zimbabwe for 20 years. He has been president of the Conference of Religious in both countries. He also works at the secretariat for formation of his own congregation, teaching formation courses in many parts of the world and doing retreat and facilitation work. He describes himself as "passionate about religious life".

Contents

Introduction

What is spirituality?

In an age in which spirituality and religion seem to mean very different things, an understanding of the term "spirituality" might prove helpful to us. We can describe spirituality as a way of living or a style of life which articulates and makes real a response to God. The starting point for a good understanding is always that it is God who initiates this relationship – God who first loved us and sent his Son to be the sacrifice which takes our sin away (1 John 4:10). Spirituality somehow draws us into a living relationship with God, which is then lived out in the context of our daily lives with ourselves and others.

A genuine spirituality integrates the whole of our lives and takes away any false divisions: "this is my time for prayer"; "this is my time for works of charity"; "this is my time for other people". A true spirituality unifies the whole of our lives, bringing into harmony one's relationship with God, with others, and with creation. An authentic spirituality, lived out in this way, shapes and transforms the whole of a person's being and experience. Any dualism from a past spirituality, dividing our lives into the sacred and the profane, has no place in contemporary spirituality.

Christian spirituality is lived in the following of Jesus of Nazareth. It embodies the very essence of his life which was a realisation of the will of the Father in the power of the Spirit. For Jesus, the will of the Father and the reign of God are at the centre of everything, giving meaning to his whole life. In him relationship with the Father, making real the reign of God in our lives and in our world are brought together in unity.

To follow Jesus means that he is "the beginning and the end", "the alpha and omega" for those seeking to live this spirituality. Those professing to live a Christian spirituality are challenged to integrate in a wholesome way their relationship with God and the actualisation of God's reign. The living out of this in the power of the Holy Spirit – through what we call "discipleship" – can then transform all our personal, communal and social relationships.

For many people an apt symbol of Christian spirituality is Mary's "yes" at the Annunciation. Mary is gripped by the Spirit, and her life is shaped and transformed. Mary's "yes" is a response of her whole being to the initiative of God: through this "yes" the Word becomes flesh in her by the power of the Spirit. Her relationship with God and her relationships with others are brought together and transformed by this experience. And we know that Mary's affirmation does not remain passive in her, but immediately becomes real and practical in the Visitation, in her care for an older woman, and then in the unfolding of the rest of her life, not only as the mother of Jesus, but as his disciple and supporter.

Spirituality of the Consecrated Life

Given that there is a Christian spirituality, is there any need of a spirituality of the consecrated life? The consecrated life is described by the documents of the Second Vatican Council as a living more deeply and radically our baptismal consecration within a given context. The Church affirms that there is indeed a specific spirituality for those living this consecrated life. It is the particular style of living the Gospel which is marked and shaped by the experience of a particular group attempting to live a specific charism within the Church: "In the Church's tradition, religious profession is considered to be a special and fruitful deepening of the consecration received in baptism". (*Vita Consecrata*, 30) In stating this, we immediately affirm that the spirituality of those living the consecrated life has no being apart from Christian spirituality. Like a member of the body in relation to the whole, it is intimately connected to Christian spirituality, yet shaped in a way that is appropriate to its particular witness.

A spirituality of the consecrated life may also be considered as a set of lived values and attitudes which give a particular flavour to the whole. It is not a recipe which one can follow blindly, but a way of life articulated in the *Constitutions* and traditions of individual religious orders and congregations. It is also shaped by, and passed on through, the lived experience of the members in mission, prayer, community, and dedication to Jesus the Redeemer: "Religious life is the following of Jesus as proposed in the Gospels." (*Perfectae Caritatis*, 2)

The *Constitutions* and *Statutes* are of course the basic texts in which the specific living out of the spirituality of the various groups is experienced. Drawing from the wells of each group's tradition, and the living witness of their membership, they shape the life of the Religious. As with the texts of scripture, however, each of the *Constitutions* cannot be understood apart from one another: they form an organic whole. A study of the individual *Constitutions* – the agreed roadmap of life for each Religious congregation or order – is essential in the attempt to rekindle the spirit given to each group.

Methodology

The method suggested for the regular gatherings is based on Saint Alphonsus' method of mental prayer. Alphonsus, a Doctor of the Church, believed that a good methodology assists in prayer and in community relationships. It is also linked to *Lectio Divina* adapted for community reflection. The approach centres on four basic steps:

- reading and studying
- meditation and reflection
- prayer and supplication
- vision and commitment

The intention is not to follow a method slavishly, but to provide an instrument that will facilitate community dialogue and give rise to a process that will overflow into our daily lives. A schema is provided for each meeting as a tool to facilitate the process of reflection.

Underlying the schema, there is also provided a series of attitudes that, since the early Church, has guided the spiritual life. All four attitudes are always present organically in our spiritual journey, although one may be more emphasised in a given moment.

This approach has a specific goal or purpose: to help us discover, as a community, what God is saying to us today, and facilitate an ever more creative response to God's Word and to our religious vocation. It presupposes a personal commitment and dedication to growth in the spiritual life. Thus it poses a challenge to each of us to examine how we are living our consecrated life.

The method proposed can be summarized with a few simple questions:

1. Reading and studying: What is the text or life experience saying? (studying and listening).
2. Meditation and reflection: What is the Lord saying to me and to the community today through this text or life experience? (reflection and dialogue).
3. Prayer and supplication: How do we respond, as individuals and community, to what the Lord is saying? (response in prayer).
4. Vision and commitment: How has the reflection and prayer in this community gathering helped us to see things as God sees them, and act as God acts? (discovery and commitment).

Mental Prayer: attitude of reflection

The first step focuses on what a text or life experience says in itself. Mental prayer leads us to ask: "What is all this saying to me and to our community? What is God saying to us through what I am experiencing?" It refers to the effort of finding the point of a given experience. As part of a method of prayer, meditation occupies a central position. As an attitude and part of a life process, it opens up new possibilities of dialogue and union. Both our minds and faulty reasoning are put at the service of our relationships. This attitude of reflection, based on listening, leads us to ask questions, to seek the sense and meaning of what is happening or being said. One way to enter into this attitude of reflection is to try to summarise briefly what has been said, read or what has happened, as part of an ongoing exchange. Through meditation, or the attitude of reflection, we permit ourselves to be transformed. Meditation as a process lets us penetrate beyond the surface of an experience or text to find the presence of the Spirit.

Prayer: attitude of responding

The first step concerns itself with what is being said, the second focuses on what this really mean to me and to the community. God is truly speaking to us. Now, in prayer, we complete the circle of dialogue: "What do I want to say? How do I want to respond to what has been said, to what has happened, to what God is saying here and now?"

As part of a spiritual process, we have been listening to what God has to say. Now is the moment to give our personal and community response to what has been experienced, to express before God what is happening within us. As an attitude, prayer is not a strict third step or logical consequence. It appears at any moment in all of our life processes. But there has to be a special time, a moment to let the heart respond to what God has said and done for us. When prayer grows into a constant attitude, it becomes like Mary's attitude when she responded: "Let what you have said be done to me." (Luke 1:38)

Prayer is realistic: it is not naive or escapist, but springs spontaneously from everyday experience, from an attitude of reading and listening critically to what is happening, from meditating and from reflecting on real life situations. This attitude of prayer expresses itself as a response of the heart or through familiar forms of prayer. It never leads us to close in on ourselves. The attitude of prayer leads the person to find, in a group or a community, the sanctuary in which to express one's true self. Furthermore, it leads the person into a commitment to empty oneself to make room for God, for one's sisters and brothers, for people who are poor or marginalised, and for the community or group I live or interact with: it moves outwards, beyond the self.

Often prayer is a spontaneous cry for help, a petition for mercy and assistance. In meditation we are confronted with our own insufficiency and sin, with our need of forgiveness. Like poor people, we become aware and express our need for God as our only source of strength and life.

Contemplation: wonder, commitment and discovery

Contemplation summarises all the previous steps. Through contemplation we can see and evaluate more clearly what has been experienced and what has happened. It gives a new vision, a new way of seeing. It develops our capacity for seeing things, people, events, as God sees them. Through this new vision we learn to see everything as a revelation of God. One learns to discover God's active, creative and redeeming presence in life and in history. To grow in this attitude is like learning to read life as if it were a book God is writing, in which we discover God's will for us.

Through the attitudes of listening, reflecting, responding in prayer, vision and commitment, we establish a process that is ever new. We never reach the point when everything is understood; we never arrive at perfect conversion. We always have before us the possibility of a deeper, more penetrating reading and understanding of life and of God's actions in our lives. There is always the hope and the prospect of listening more closely, of reflecting more deeply, of a prayer that is more profoundly committed to love, of a more transparent contemplation.

The attitude of contemplation permits us to see reality more clearly. It opens up possibilities for a deeper love and of changing what is not according to God's will. St. Alphonsus, in *The Need for Mental Prayer*, says that mental prayer brings us before a mirror, where we can see ourselves as we are, and are then capable of changing what has to be changed. Likewise, St Bernard says that prayer is like a mirror: if someone has a blemish on his face, he goes before a mirror, sees it and removes it; otherwise, the blemish stays there and always remains because he cannot see it and thus does not remove it. Something like this happens in prayer. If one has a fault, if one is in a difficult situation, one goes to prayer and there, suddenly, as before a mirror, we see in our own conscience that defect, perhaps that sin, that danger of losing God, and we act accordingly.

The word "mirroring" is of course a very Pauline concept (2 Corinthians 3:18). St. Paul would hold that this "seeing" transforms our lives. It leads to a renewed commitment, to resolutions that give expression to what has been experienced. Our lives become more and more a living Gospel. It is akin to God's word: it says and it does. It is the Holy Spirit that moves us to live an ever deeper expression of gratitude to God's love.

Session One

The Mind and Heart of the Consecrated Person

Theme: The wonder and joy of our vocation.

Aspects: The call of Jesus; his journey; our lives; our journey.

Texts for orientation

"Yes, God loved the world so much
that he gave his only Son,
so that everyone who believes in him may not be lost
but may have eternal life." (John 3:16)

[Religious life] "is a privileged witness to a constant seeking for God, an undivided love for Jesus Christ and an absolute dedication to the growth of his kingdom." (Pope Paul VI, *Evangelica Testificatio, Apostolic Exhortation on the Renewal of Religious Life*, 3)

Introduction

A copy of the *Constitutions*, which are in reality the road map of the journey for any consecrated life, is placed on a small table in the centre of the group. Perhaps also a poster or a picture of a road or a path leading into the distance is placed there, to symbolise the journeys of those who have gone before us and our own journey through life.

The community prays in silence

The community prays together in silence to the Holy Spirit for guidance on this personal and shared journey. After an adequate time of silent, personal prayer, the community prays the *Our Father* together. A hymn or appropriate song may also be used instead.

Lived experience

It appears that from the beginning, those called by the Lord were seized with an individual and focused love for the person of Jesus. With this, each one began a new journey, which led to a discovery of what was at the very heart of Jesus. For these men and women this became an overriding desire to experience the burning heat of the Father's love in the person of Jesus, who had touched their hearts.

You are invited to share with the community (or if on private retreat to recall) your own personal journey to your order or congregation.

- How did you come to be a religious in this particular group?
- Why do you remain a religious?

Where is your present journey leading you:

- In terms of your relationship with Jesus?
- In terms of being a "spirit filled evangelizer"?
  (Pope Francis, *Evangelii Gaudium*, 262)
- In terms of self sacrifice for the salvation of the world, especially for "the liberation and promotion of the poor"? (*Evangelii Gaudium*, 187)
- In terms of being filled "with a joy ever new"? (*Evangelii Gaudium*, 1)

Share your reflections with the community.

The Word of God

Let us now listen together to Acts 9:1-9, the story of Saul's conversion.

Meanwhile Saul was still breathing threats to slaughter the Lord's disciples. He had gone to the high priests and asked for letters addressed to the synagogues in Damascus that would authorise him to arrest any followers of the Way, men or women, that he could find.

Suddenly, while he was travelling to Damascus and just before he reached the city, there came a light from heaven all round him. He fell to the ground and then he heard a voice saying, "Saul, Saul, why are you persecuting me?" "Who are you, Lord?" he asked, and the voice answered, "I am Jesus, and you are persecuting me. Get up and go into the city, and you will be told what you have to do." The men travelling with Saul stood there speechless, for though they heard the voice they could see no one. Saul got up from the ground, but even with his eyes wide open he could see nothing at all, and they had to lead him into Damascus by the hand. For three days he was without his sight, and took neither food nor drink.

The reading should be done slowly, clearly, with a short period of silence after it is finished. It can be read two or more times, so that the words stay in our hearts and minds.

- What strikes you most about this encounter?
- What is the significance of the Lord's question?
- Where does this encounter lead Saul?

Meditation and reflection

Let us now consider what God is saying to us in what we have shared so far.

- What does the reading from Acts say to you personally and to us as a community?
- Describe a time when you felt the power of Jesus seize you so that you were able to say a generous "yes" to God.
- Describe a dark moment in your journey which you now perceive as a moment of grace.

Prayer and supplication

God is speaking to us. After sharing our life experience and reflecting on the word, we now take time to respond in prayer to what the Lord is saying to us. We let our hearts respond to God.

Together let us pray these verses from Psalm 139:

O Lord, you search me and you know me,
you know my resting and my rising,
you discern my purpose from afar.
You mark when I walk or lie down,
all my ways lie open to you.

Before ever a word is on my tongue
you know it, O Lord, through and through.
Behind and before you besiege me,
your hand ever laid upon me.
Too wonderful for me, this knowledge,
too high, beyond my reach.

O where can I go from your spirit,
or where can I flee from your face?
If I climb the heavens, you are there.
If I lie in the grave, you are there.
If I take the wings of the dawn
and dwell at the sea's furthest end,
even there your hand would lead me,
your right hand would hold me fast.

If I say: "Let the darkness hide me
and the light around me be night,
even darkness is not dark for you
and the night is as clear as the day.

For it was you who created my being,
knit me together in my mother's womb.
I thank you for the wonder of my being,
for the wonders of all your creation.

Already you knew my soul,
my body held no secret from you
when I was being fashioned in secret
and moulded in the depths of the earth.

Your eyes saw all my actions,
they were all of them written in your book;
every one of my days was decreed
before one of them came into being.

To me, how mysterious your thoughts,
the sum of them not to be numbered!
If I count them, they are more than the sand;
to finish, I must be eternal, like you.

O search me, God, and know my heart.
O test me and know my thoughts.
See that I follow not the wrong path
and lead me in the path of life eternal.

Each member may choose a verse which applies to his or her life's journey and silently pray about it in their hearts for a few moments. Any member may express their prayer out loud.

Sharing vision and resolutions

We are setting out together through this experience on a journey of renewal and rededication to our consecrated life.

- What have we "seen" and understood as a result of our reflection or our sharing today?
- From what we have dialogued and prayed about, what obstacles have you discovered that we need to deal with personally and as a community before we journey? How can we help each other to make this journey fruitful and effective?
- What commitment can we now make personally and as a community in order to live this journey in good faith?

Preparation for the next meeting

Arrange the date and time of the next meeting and invite a member of the group to co-ordinate it and prepare its final celebration.

Celebration

Celebrate the life of your Founder/Foundress either with a short para-liturgy highlighting some particular aspect of his or her life or a reading from one of his or her letters, and then share a meal or other community celebration.

Session Two

The Response of the Consecrated Person – Yes! Yes! Yes!

Theme: Our "yes" is rooted in baptism and deepened by religious profession.

Aspects: We are changed radically through baptism which is the core of our vocation.

Texts for orientation

"You are my Son, the Beloved; my favour rests on you." (Mark 1:11)

"Christ is the seal on our foreheads; he is the seal on our hearts: on the forehead because we always profess him; on the heart because we always love him; he is the seal on our arms because we are always working for him. Consecrated life is in fact a continuous call to follow Christ and to be made like him." (*Rejoice, A Message from the Teachings of Pope Francis*, Congregation for Institutes of Consecrated Life and Societies of Apostolic Life, 2014, 5)

"The first duty of the consecrated life is to make visible the marvels wrought by God in the frail humanity of those who are called. They bear witness to these marvels not so much in words as by the eloquent language of a transfigured life, capable of amazing the world. (*Vita Consecrata*, 20)

Introduction

A bowl of water, which will be used for the renewal of baptismal promises, and the *Formula of Profession* are placed on the table together with a painting or image of Jesus the Redeemer. An appropriate song or hymn (about living water or new life) is sung. (During a private retreat, read Isaiah 55: 1-3.) A member of the community says a prayer to the Holy Spirit asking for light and guidance.

Lived experience

We are called to continue what *Vita Consecrata* calls "a transfigured life" in a radical way.

* In what way are you radical at a personal or community level? What ways could you be more radical?
* What is the greatest challenge faced by religious in today's world? How can I/we begin to respond to it?
* The vowed life calls us personally and as a community to be transformed, and to be a living witness of Jesus. What structures do we need to put in place, change, or remove, so that we can be more credible living witnesses of Jesus in our society?

Word of God

Let us now read John 1:35-39.

On the following day as John stood there again with two of his disciples, Jesus passed, and John stared hard at him and said, "Look, there is the lamb of God." Hearing this, the two disciples followed Jesus. Jesus turned round, saw them following and said, "What do you want?" They answered, "Rabbi," – which means "Teacher" – "where do you live?" "Come and see," he replied; so they went and saw where he lived, and stayed with him the rest of that day. It was about the tenth hour.

The reading should be done slowly and meditatively with a short period of silence after it is finished.

* What does this text mean to you? Share this with the group.
* "They stayed with him the rest of that day." In our religious life, is spending a day with the Lord part of our monthly plan or our daily attitude?
* Evaluate the authenticity of your/our daily lifestyle.
* "We are victims of this culture of the temporary. I would like you to think about this: how can I be free, how can I break free from this culture of the temporary?" (Pope Francis, *Address to Novices and Seminarians*, 6 July 2013)

Meditation and reflection

As we reflect on the wonder of our call to be credible religious in today's world, we need to ask:

- What more do I need to leave behind in order to follow Jesus more closely?
- What are the personal and community obstacles which inhibit a total and complete response to our call in "the following of Jesus as proposed by the Gospel"? (*Perfectae Caritatis*, 2)

Prayer and supplication

God speaks to us in many ways. At times it is through a challenge, an invitation, even his silent glance. "Look into the depth of your heart, look into your own inner depth and ask yourself: do you have a heart that desires something great, or a heart that has been lulled to sleep by things?" (Pope Francis, *Address to General Chapter of the Augustinians* (28 August 2013)

- The "Second Summons" is the call often received in middle or later life to renew radically our hearts and commitment. Am I courageous enough to listen for this call?
- The challenge of Pope Francis is to "enter into intimacy with Christ and bear fruit. Remain in Jesus! This means remaining attached to him, in him, with him, talking to him." (*Rejoice*, 5)
- Do we make enough quality time to discern truly what is being asked of us?

Sharing vision and resolutions

Religious life is a daily call to enter more deeply into the heart of Jesus. As with the apostles, and even with those who have gone before us, this is a process of gradual growth as individuals and as a community.

- Are there ways in which we can encourage this ideal, and renew our personal and community enthusiasm for our vocation at the heart of the Church?
- The Spirit makes us signs, witnesses, and even now sharers of "a new heaven and a new earth" (Revelation 21:1). In what ways can we, especially as religious, be more credible witnesses to the enduring love of God in our increasingly secularised world?
- We now make the sign of the cross on our forehead and quietly renew our baptismal promises.

Preparation for the next meeting

Arrange the date and the time for the next meeting, and invite a member of the community to coordinate it and prepare the final celebration.

Celebration

Place the names of all the jubilarians for this year on the table. Celebrate them, and all who have gone before us in the community, with deep gratitude. Raise a glass to them!

Proclaimers of the Gospel

Theme: Being evangelists by our words and lifestyle.

Aspects: Pastoral activity; the heart of the Gospel; encounter with those in need.

Texts for orientation

"Go out to the whole world; proclaim the Good News to all creation." (Mark: 16:16)

"Not that I do boast of preaching the Gospel, since it is a duty that has been laid upon me." (1 Corinthians 9:16)

"The sense of mission is at the very heart of consecrated life." (*Vita Consecrata*, 41)

"All of us are asked to obey his call to go forth from our own comfort zone in order to reach all the 'peripheries' in need of the light of the Gospel." (*Evangelii Gaudium*, 20)

Introduction

On the table place a Book of the Gospels, and two maps, one showing your local area and the other, a world map. If possible also place a copy of *Ad Gentes*, the *Decree on the Church's Missionary Activity*.

Lived experience

By living our baptism at a radical level we are called to be apostles of the word of God, witnessing to it, and sharing it by word and deed. This is at the heart of our consecration. This involves some closeness with the people of God. "Evangelizers thus take on the 'smell of the sheep' and the sheep listen to their voice." (*Evangelii Gaudium*, 24)

- Do we seek out opportunities to proclaim the word in an explicit manner – whether formally or informally? Are we comfortable and confident enough to proclaim the name of Jesus?
- Do our lives as a community and our personal lifestyles offer true witness to the Gospel? Are we prepared to leave our comfort zones in order to be truly missionary, no matter where we are?
- Sickness, incapacity and old age can be powerful witnesses of fidelity as well as enabling us to continue to be truly missionary in our society. Do we appreciate this for others and for ourselves?

The word of God, especially as proclaimed in the Gospel, is the whole basis for our missionary life as consecrated persons. Unless we are steeped in the Gospel message, we will not have the energy or the courage to proclaim it.

Let us listen to Matthew 28:16-20.

Meanwhile the eleven disciples set out for Galilee, to the mountain where Jesus had arranged to meet them. When they saw him they fell down before him, though some hesitated. Jesus came up and spoke to them. He said, "All authority in heaven and on earth has been given to me. Go, therefore, make disciples of all the nations; baptise them in the name of the Father and of the Son and of the Holy Spirit, and teach them to observe all the commands I gave you. And know that I am with you always; yes, to the end of time.

And from Acts 2: 1-4.

When Pentecost day came round, they had all met in one room, when suddenly they heard what sounded like a powerful wind from heaven, the noise of which filled the entire house in which they were sitting; and something appeared to them that seemed like tongues of fire; these separated and came to rest on the head of each of them. They were all filled with the Holy Spirit, and began to speak foreign languages as the Spirit gave them the gift of speech.

- Do we share the Gospel in any real sense? Are we able to offer an opportunity for scripture study or shared prayer to others? Do we evangelise one another?
- How do we practise and witness to the social dimensions of the Gospel?
- Are we prepared to attempt a new closeness to the people in order to be more effective evangelists?

Meditation and reflection

"We are called to undertake an exodus out of our own selves, setting out on a path of adoration and service. 'We must go out through the door to seek and meet the people' … I would like you to be almost obsessed about this. Be so, without being presumptuous." (Pope Francis, *Rejoice*, 10)

- Our life of prayer is meant to be at the service of our missionary endeavours. The invitation of prayer is to pour out our lives in service of the world.
- In his *Exhortation*, Pope Francis invites us to prepare for evangelisation by "personalising the word"; "having reverence for the truth"; "spiritual reading" and by having "an ear for the people" (*Evangelii Gaudium*, 3). Discuss this.
- "In obedience to Christ's commandment, is the missionary drive *ad gentes*, which every committed Christian shares with the Church… This drive is felt above all by members of institutes whether of the contemplative or active life" (*Vita Consecrata*, 77). How energised are we by the Gospel message?

Prayer and supplication

"Spirit-filled evangelisers are evangelisers who pray and work" (Pope Francis, *Rejoice*, 262). All missionary activities will be only a series of good works unless carried out in the Spirit of Jesus.

- Our varied ministries will only be effective if they are carried out in the power of the Spirit. Can we commit ourselves to more focused prayer in this area?
- A huge part of preparation for any apostolic activity is a correspondingly serious commitment to seek the assistance of the Lord Jesus.
- "The primary reason for evangelizing is the love of Jesus which we have received and the power of salvation which urges us to ever greater love of him" (*Evangelii Gaudium*, 264). Is this really true for us and for me?

Sharing vision and resolutions

Taking the ideas of Pope Francis in *Evangelii Gaudium* as a challenge, we reflect on the following:

- Person to person. "Being a disciple means constantly being ready to bring the love of Jesus to others, and this can happen unexpectedly and in any place: on the street, in a city square, during work, on a journey." (*Evangelii Gaudium*, 127)
  How vigilant am I for such opportunities, and how can I/we be more open to them?
- The evangelizing power of popular piety. Are we open to the ordered devotions of the culture and ambience in which we live? "Herein lies the importance of popular piety, a true expression of the spontaneous missionary activity of the people of God." (*Evangelii Gaudium*, 122)
  Discuss both traditional and modern expression of piety.
- Words which set hearts on fire. What structures can we put in place which will be a seedbed for a new evangelisation that captures the hearts of the hearers?
- "We are all missionary disciples. We need to evangelize, but also allow ourselves to be constantly evangelized." (*Evangelii Gaudium*, 121)
  What opportunities can we create for this experience?

Preparation for the next meeting

Arrange the date and the time for the next meeting, and invite a member of the community to coordinate it and prepare the final celebration.

Celebration

To conclude, make a positive intention to pray for a specific missionary task over the next month. Have some snacks together and recall some of your missionary activities.

Personal Reflection

JESUS SAID "THE WATER THAT

Session Four

Captivated by Love

Theme: Chastity – a response of love.

Aspects: The power of love; the life-giving nature of love; the witness of love.

Texts for orientation

"Happy the pure in heart:
they shall see God." (Matthew 5:8)

"The consecrated life witnesses to the power of God's love manifest in the weakness of the human condition. The consecrated person attests that what many have believed impossible becomes, with the Lord's grace, possible and truly liberating. Yes, in Christ it is possible to love God with all one's heart, putting him above every other love, and thus to love every creature with the freedom of God!... It is a witness which also meets a growing need for interior honesty in human relationships." (*Vita Consecrata*, 88)

Introduction

An icon of *Jesus the Redeemer*, a candle and the *Constitutions* are placed on a table. One of the members leads the group by praying the prayer of Christ in John 17:17-24.

> Consecrate them in the truth;
> your word is truth.
> As you sent me into the world,
> I have sent them into the world,
> and for their sake I consecrate myself
> so that they too may be consecrated in truth.
> I pray not only for these,
> but for those also
> who through their words will believe in me.
> May they all be one.
> Father, may they be one in us,
> as you are in me and I am in you,
> so that the world may believe it was you who sent me.
> I have given them the glory you gave to me,
> that they may be one as we are one.
> With me in them and you in me,
> may they be so completely one
> that the world will realise that it was you who sent me
> and that I have loved them as much as you loved me.
> Father,
> I want those you have given me
> to be with me where I am,
> so that they may always see the glory
> you have given me
> because you loved me
> before the foundation of the world.

Lived experience

- How has your view of chastity enabled you to develop your human and emotional life, and get in touch with your deepest passion?
- Describe how you have been able to develop real friendships within and outside the community, friendships which have enhanced your vocation.
- How can your community foster a greater atmosphere of human living and intimacy, while remaining a truly religious house focused on God?

Word of God

Let us now read the text of Ephesians 3:14-21.

This, then, is what I pray, kneeling before the Father, from whom every family, whether spiritual or natural, takes its name:

Out of his infinite glory, may he give you the power through his Spirit for your hidden self to grow strong, so that Christ may live in your hearts through faith, and then, planted in love and built on love, you will with all the saints have strength to grasp the breadth and the length, the height and the depth; until knowing the love of Christ, which is beyond all knowledge, you are filled with the utter fullness of God.

Glory be to him whose power, working in us, can do infinitely more than we can ask or imagine; glory be to him from generation to generation in the Church and in Christ Jesus for ever and ever. Amen.

The reading should be done meditatively. Afterwards, those who wish may echo a key phrase from the text. Share with the group what moved you in this text and why.

Meditation and reflection

"In calling you, God says to you, 'You are important to me, I love you, I am counting on you.' Jesus says this to each one of us! Joy is born from that! The joy of the moment that Jesus looked at me. Understanding and hearing this is the secret of our joy. Feeling loved by God, feeling that for him we are not numbers, but people; and we know that it is he who is calling us." (Pope Francis, *Address to Novices and Seminarians*, 7 July 2013)

"The consecrated life must present to today's world examples of chastity lived by men and woman who show balance, self-mastery, an enterprising spirit, and psychological and affective maturity." (*Vita Consecrata*, 88)

"It was I who begot you in Christ Jesus by preaching the Good News."
(1 Corinthians 4:15)

- How may we enter more fully into this mystery of love, and create an atmosphere in which this simplicity of relationship may be deepened?
- Is our community a place in which true human warmth, as well as a lively spiritual desire, can be lived and shared at a deep and real level?
- In the face of the sexual scandals in the Church and in religious life, how can we show a face of wholeness to our society?

Prayer and supplication

Real love is at the very heart of the different charisms contained in our religious lives.

- "As the Father has loved me,
  so I have loved you.
  Remain in my love." (John 15:9)
- "In the evening of your life you will be judged on the amount of love you have put into it." (St John of the Cross)
- Repeat the phrase, "My God, you are love", as you breathe in. Then, as you breathe out, whisper, "Make me truly loving." Do this slowly and rhythmically for some minutes.

Sharing vision and resolutions

The Gospels and the documents of the Church present us with the challenge of being really in touch with our human emotions and affections, yet not being ruled by them.

- Reflect on how you maintain this balance in your own life.
- In the past chastity was seen negatively as the Old Testament mandate of, "Thou shalt not...", rather than as the New Testament promise of, "How happy are those ..." How may we reflect this in a society which sees sex as a commodity, and relationships as transient?
- The aim of entering into a covenant union with God through the vow of chastity is a desire for real union, for actual communion. Have we lost that desire, or see it as beyond us?
- This gift of union remains an offer from God. Are our hearts open enough to receive it?

Preparation for the next meeting

Arrange the date and the time for the next meeting, and invite a member of the community to coordinate it and prepare the final celebration.

Celebration

The gift of a loving relationship demands a celebration. Arrange a community meal or a party in which you celebrate your common calling to be consecrated people who are in love with God and with life.

Praying in the Spirit

Theme: Men and women of prayer; communities of prayer.

Aspects: Our life-line with God; our nourishment; pouring out our lives for others.

Texts for orientation

"Then he told them a parable about the need to pray continually and never lose heart." (Luke 18:1)

"In your prayers do not babble as the pagans do, for they think that by using many words they will make themselves heard." (Matthew 6:7)

"The interior journey begins with prayer. The first thing for a disciple is to be with the Master, to listen to him, and to learn from him. This is always true, and it is true at every moment of our lives… If the warmth of God, of his love, of his tenderness is not in our own hearts, then how can we, who are poor sinners, warm the hearts of others?" (Pope Francis, *Rejoice*, 6)

"The call to holiness is accepted and can be cultivated only in the silence of adoration before the infinite transcendent God… In practice this involves great fidelity to liturgical and personal prayers, to periods devoted to mental prayer and contemplation, to Eucharistic adoration, to monthly retreats and spiritual exercises." (*Vita Consecrata*, 38)

Introduction

On the table place the *Bible*, the *Liturgy of the Hours* and, if possible, some liturgical symbols such as bread and wine. Invite a member of the community to ask the Holy Spirit to pray for us, through us, and in us in the meeting.

Lived experience

Being a religious means being a man or woman of the liturgy. Here, we are united in a special way with the prayer of Jesus to the Father. This is especially true in terms of the celebration of the sacraments and praying the Liturgy of the Hours.

- Are we, as Christians living our baptismal dedication more radically, conscious of the invitation to celebrate this public prayer of praise and intercession in the name of all humanity?
- Down through the ages, the Eucharist and the Blessed Sacrament have been at the heart of the lives of religious. What does this mean in my/our day-to-day lives?
- Personal prayer, lived in a climate of intimacy with the Lord, is at the heart of all our vocations, inviting us into true mystical union with Jesus.
- Does the community, or do I, create an atmosphere in which various forms of "silent contemplation" are possible, thereby enabling us to have a personal experience of God?

Word of God

"The word of God is the first source of all Christian spirituality. It gives rise to a personal relationship with the living God and with his saving and sanctifying will."
(*Vita Consecrata*, 94)

Let us now read Matthew 18:19-20.

I tell you solemnly once again, if two of you on earth agree to ask anything at all, it will be granted to you by my Father in heaven. For where two or three meet in my name, I shall be there with them.

And from Romans 8:26-28.

The Spirit too comes to help us in our weakness. For when we cannot choose words in order to pray properly, the Spirit himself expresses our plea in a way that could never be put into words, and God who knows everything in our hearts knows perfectly well what he means, and that the pleas of the saints expressed by the Spirit are according to the mind of God.

Please read these scriptural texts slowly and meditatively.

- What is our belief about the power of prayer in our lives and in our community?
- How can we be more attentive to the call of the Spirit in our personal and community listening?

Meditation and reflection

"It is therefore of great benefit for consecrated persons to meditate regularly on the Gospel texts and the New Testament writings which describe the words and example of Jesus Christ." (*Vita Consecrata*, 94)

- How do I nourish myself with the word of God and with other quality spiritual reading each day? Use a favourite text from scripture, and repeat it over and over again today.
- The life of a consecrated man or woman is a life of the praise of God. Spend some time in praise and adoration.
- Use a mantra, such as "Maranatha – Come Lord Jesus", in these prayer moments.

Prayer and supplication

"Drawing on the authentic sources of Christian spirituality, let the members of communities energetically cultivate the spirit of prayer and the practise of it." (*Lumen Gentium*, 6)

- Intercessory prayer is part of being human in the face of God. How can we make this more authentic and less of a routine habit?
- Praise and thanksgiving are at the heart of prayer. Is there space in my life or in our lives for expressing our gratitude to God?

Sharing vision and resolutions

- Study is an often neglected, but utterly important part of the prayer life of a disciple of Jesus. What time do we set aside for focused study in an area of, for example, the scriptures, theology, liturgy, spirituality?
- Retreats and days of recollection were previously written into the fabric of religious life. Do we make time at least on one day a month and for a number of days each year to spend a day with the Lord? (John 1:39)
- Are these really times of deep listening and self-emptying in order to be filled with the Spirit? Or do we perhaps avoid the real face-to-face encounter with God in silence and in the desert?

- "Special devotions" are recommended, such as the Rosary, the Way of the Cross, and various novenas. How can we develop these in meaningful, contemporary and cultural ways?

Preparation for the next meeting

Arrange the date and the time for the next meeting, and invite a member of the community to coordinate it and prepare the final celebration.

Celebration

To conclude, put the names of all the members of the community, or of the Province, in a basket, and at random pick the name of one you will pray for especially during the coming month. Have a cup of coffee or a glass of wine together.

Personal Reflection

To Live and to Die for Jesus

Theme: Continual conversion and repentance.

Aspects: Bearing in our bodies the agony of Jesus; being docile to the Spirit.

Texts for orientation

"If anyone wants to be a follower of mine, let him renounce himself and take up his cross every day and follow me." (Luke 9:23)

"Anyone who loves his life loses it;
anyone who hates his life in this world
will keep it for the eternal life." (John 12:25)

"To persevere all the way to Golgotha, to experience the lacerations of doubt and denial, to rejoice in the marvel and wonder of the Paschal event, up to the manifestation of Pentecost and the evangelisation of the peoples, these are the milestones of joyful fidelity because they are about self-emptying, experienced throughout life, even in the sign of martyrdom, and also sharing the life of the risen Christ. And it is from the Cross, the supreme act of mercy and love, that we are reborn as a new creation."
(Pope Francis, *Address to Novices and Seminarians*, 7 July 2013)

"When we journey without the Cross, when we build without the Cross, when we profess Christ without the Cross, we are not disciples of the Lord, we are worldly."
(Pope Francis, *Homily at Mass*, 14 March 2013)

Introduction

A crucifix should be placed on the table, and a candle. As the candle is lit, the community prays together Psalm 51 – the *Miserere*.

Have mercy on me, God, in your kindness.
In your compassion blot out my offence.
O wash me more and more from my guilt
and cleanse me from my sin.

My offences truly I know them;
my sin is always before me.
Against you, you alone, have I sinned;
what is evil in your sight I have done.

That you may be justified when you give sentence
and be without reproach when you judge.
O see, in guilt was I born,
a sinner was I conceived.

Indeed you love truth in the heart;
then in the secret of my heart teach me wisdom.
O purify me, then I shall be clean;
O wash me, I shall be whiter than snow.

Make me hear rejoicing and gladness,
that the bones you have crushed may revive.
From my sins turn away your face
and blot out all my guilt.

A pure heart create for me, O God,
put a steadfast spirit within me.
Do not cast me away from your presence,
nor deprive me of your holy spirit.

Give me again the joy of your help;
with a spirit of fervour sustain me,
that I may teach transgressors your ways
and sinners may return to you.

O rescue me, God, my helper,
and my tongue shall ring out your goodness.

O Lord, open my lips
and my mouth shall declare your praise.

For in sacrifice you take no delight,
burnt offering from me you would refuse;
my sacrifice, a contrite spirit.
A humbled, contrite heart you will not spurn.

In your goodness, show favour to Zion:
rebuild the walls of Jerusalem.
Then you will be pleased with lawful sacrifice,
holocausts offered on your altar.

Lived Experience

- In the act of our religious profession we made a complete gift of our lives to God. We entered into the mystery of the *kenosis* – the self-emptying of Jesus. Are we living what we promised individually and as a community?
- Daily conversion is the way to have the "new heart" promised in the scriptures. What do you understand by "daily conversion"?
- Conversion takes place sacramentally when we seek reconciliation in the sacrament. It also takes place personally and in community. How, in reality can this occur?

Word of God

Let us now read Philippians 3:7-13.

But because of Christ, I have come to consider all these advantages that I had as disadvantages. Not only that, but I believe nothing can happen that can outweigh the supreme advantage of knowing Christ Jesus my Lord. For him I have accepted the loss of everything, and I look on everything as so much rubbish if only I can have Christ and be given a place in him. I am no longer trying for perfection by my own efforts, the perfection that comes from the Law, but I want only the perfection that comes through faith in Christ, and is from God and based on faith. All I want is to know Christ and the power of his resurrection and to share his sufferings by reproducing the pattern of his death. That is the way I can hope to take my place in the resurrection of the dead. Not that I have become perfect yet: I have not yet won, but I am still running, trying to capture the prize for which Christ Jesus captured me. I can assure you my brothers, I am far from thinking I have already won. All I can say is that I forget the past and I strain ahead for what is still to come.

- Do we really live these beautiful words?
- Do we try to count the love of Jesus Christ as the one thing for which we are prepared to lose everything?
- Share with the group your hopes and struggles in connection with this.

Meditation and reflection

"Yet he did not cling to his equality with God but emptied himself to assume the condition of a slave." (Philippians 2:6-7)

"What am I to do with you, Ephraim?
What am I to do with you, Judah?
This love of yours is like a morning cloud,
like the dew that quickly disappears." (Hosea 6:4)

"Come back to me with all your heart." (Joel 2:12)

"All human beings are thus confronted with their condition as sinners, and with their need for penitence and conversion." (St John Paul II, General Audience, Ash Wednesday 2001)

Use the texts above for individual and community reflection and sharing.

Prayer and supplication

"Consecrated persons discover that the more they stand at the foot of the Cross of Christ, the more immediately and profoundly they experience the truth of God who is love" (*Vita Consecrata*, 24). This challenge calls for a true self-awareness – and also the ability to "hear" others, especially those in authority, as they invite us to greater spiritual and human growth.

- Pray for docility, and also for the courage to accept, even in "serene fidelity" (*Vita Consecrata*, 24), that inner daily conversion which is necessary for the authentic living of our vocation.
- Pray "Put a new heart within me", or "Lord Jesus be merciful to me a sinner", quietly and repetitively.

Sharing vision and resolutions

"Salvation is therefore, and above all, redemption from sin, which hinders friendship with God, a liberation from the state of slavery in which we find ourselves ever since we succumbed to the temptation of the Evil One and lost the freedom of the children of God (cf. Romans 8:21)." (St John Paul ll, *Misericordia Dei*, 2)

- The sacrament of reconciliation can be so difficult in terms of its repetitiveness. Yet it is the sacrament of constant renewal. How can we prepare more effectively to receive the grace of this special moment?
- Personal and community acts of penance are still necessary in our Church today. Self-emptying in terms of fasting and making Friday a special day of penance are both recommended by the Church. What practical personal and community acts can we use?

Preparation for the next meeting

Arrange the date and the time for the next meeting, and invite a member of the community to coordinate it and prepare the final celebration.

Celebration

The meeting ends with an exchange of the sign of peace – and then a simple celebration.

Session Seven

Brothers and Sisters Together

Theme: Our life in community.

Aspects: Fostering relationships; responsibility; initiatives; personal choice.

Texts for orientation

"All I have is yours
and all you have is mine,
and in them I am glorified.
I am not in the world any longer,
but they are in the world,
and I am coming to you.
Holy Father,
keep those you have given me true to your name,
so that they may be one like us." (John 17:10-11)

"Community is the first and most believable gospel we can preach. We are asked to humanise our community. Build friendship between yourselves... There are and there will be problems but... search for a solution with love. Build community... and community life with a big heart. Let things go, do not brag, be patient with everything, smile from the heart." (Pope Francis, *Rejoice*, 9)

Introduction

A copy of the *Constitutions* is placed on the table, and also a list of the names of all the members of the community – perhaps also with a photograph of each one.

Lived Experience

"The communitarian ideal must not blind us to the fact that every Christian reality is built on human frailty. The perfect 'ideal community' does not exist yet; the perfect communion of saints is our goal in the heavenly Jerusalem."
(Congregation for Consecrated Life, *Fraternal Life in Community*, 26)

Living in community is at times experienced as a blessing, at times as a difficulty or a trial.

- Describe your happiest time in the community. What made it happy?
- Think of times in community when you have not been able to celebrate the reality of community life. What was going on inside you at this time? What was going on in the community at this time?
- What realistically do you expect from community, and what have you to offer to your present community?

The Word of God

Let us now read the text of Colossians 3:12-17 on the call to community.

You are God's chosen race, his saints; he loves you, and you should be clothed in sincere compassion, in kindness and humility, gentleness and patience. Bear with one another; forgive each other as soon as a quarrel begins. The Lord has forgiven you; now you must do the same. Over all these clothes, to keep them and complete them, put on love. And may the peace of Christ reign in your hearts, because it is for this that you were called together as parts of one body. Always be thankful.
    Let the message of Christ, in all its richness, find a home with you. Teach each other, and advise each other, in all wisdom. With gratitude in your hearts sing psalm and hymns and inspired songs to God; and never say or do anything except in the name of the Lord Jesus, giving thanks to God the Father through him.

Read this slowly and meditatively.

- What is at the centre of Paul's challenge in this text?
- How can we make it realistic and practical?

Meditation and reflection

"Religious community is the place where the daily and patient passage from 'me' to 'us' takes place; from my commitment to a commitment entrusted to the community; from seeking 'my things' to seeking 'the things of Christ.'"
(Congregation for Consecrated Life, *Fraternal Life in Community*, 39)

- What is God asking me to offer to the community, and what is God asking me to surrender?
- How flexible am I in my attitude to others?
- Am I able to see the good in each community member?
- Hold each member of the community individually before God: name one of their gifts and celebrate it.

Prayer and supplication

God calls us to be part of one body – our religious community. This is a gift. Let us thank God by echoing Paul's hymn of gratitude in Ephesians 1:3-6.

Blessed be God the Father of our Lord Jesus Christ,
who has blessed us with all the spiritual blessings of heaven in Christ.
Before the world was made, he chose us, chose us in Christ,
to be holy and spotless, and to live through love in his presence,
determining that we should become his adopted sons, through Jesus Christ
for his own kind purposes,
to make us praise the glory of his grace,
his free gift to us in the Beloved.

After the reading, anyone may offer a prayer of thanksgiving.

Sharing vision and resolutions

"Because religious community is a *Schola Amoris* which help one to grow in love for God and for one's brothers and sisters, it is also a place for human growth."
(Congregation for Consecrated Life, *Fraternal Life in Community*, 35)

Human growth involves interaction and dialogue, and also being part of a community which is in permanent formation. There are major challenges of freedom, identity, authority and psychological maturity. These can only be worked at as a "symphony" in which there is mutual respect and focused listening.

- How do we celebrate the individual gifts and cultural differences that are part of today's religious life?
- In what way can we respect "the slower journey of weaker members without stifling the growth of richer personalities"? (*Fraternal Life in Community*, 40)
- How can we retain unity in our new found diversity?

"We stay together in community not because we have chosen one another, but because we have been chosen by the Lord." (*Fraternal Life in Community*, 41)
Reflect on this statement.

Preparation for the next meeting

Arrange the date and the time for the next meeting, and invite a member of the community to coordinate it and prepare the final celebration.

Celebration

Have a community party – and enjoy "wasting time" with each other.

Personal Reflection

Living in Joy

Theme: The joy of the Gospel.

Aspects: Living in love; happiness and the Gospels; a joy ever new.

Texts for orientation

"I have told you this
so that my own joy may be in you
and your joy may be complete." (John 15:11)

"Did not our hearts burn within us as he talked to us on the road and explained the scriptures to us?" (Luke 24:32)

"The joy of the Gospel fills the hearts and lives of all who encounter Jesus. Those who accept his offer of salvation are set free from sin, sorrow, inner emptiness and loneliness. With Christ joy is constantly born anew." (Pope Francis, *Rejoice*, 1)

"A joyful heart is the normal result of a heart burning with love. She gives most who gives with joy." (Blessed Teresa of Calcutta)

"What in people's eyes can seem a waste is, for the individuals captivated in the depth of their heart by the beauty and goodness of the Lord, an obvious response of love, a joyful expression of gratitude for having been admitted in a unique way to the knowledge of the Son and to a sharing in his mission in this world."(*Vita Consecrata*, 104)

Introduction

On a table place the Bible and some symbols which capture a sense of beauty. These could include a plant, a picture or an icon. Pray that we may recognise beauty in our world, our lives and those of our group.

Lived experience

Pope Francis has invited all who live the consecrated life to reclaim a sense of true joy. This is a Gospel invitation which has been present since the time of Jesus. The experience of this has, however, been lost at certain times with an over emphasis on suffering and the cross. A balance is needed. We are invited to experience and live the joy of the Gospel.

- We are challenged not to be "like someone who has just come back from a funeral" but to be people "whose lives glow with fervour and who have first received the joy of Christ" (*Evangelii Gaudium*, 10). The image of the consecrated life has at times been perceived negatively. How can we witness as individuals and communities to the joy of the Lord in an authentic manner?
- Joy comes from a fulfilled life, from "concentrating on the essentials, on what is most beautiful, most grand, most appealing, and at the same time most necessary" (*Evangelii Gaudium*, 10). How can we seek out truth and beauty which will lead to real joy? How can we make time for the one thing necessary? (See Luke 10:41-42)

The Word of God

The New Testament is an invitation to live in the joy of the risen Jesus. Let us listen to these short texts which might encourage us to a greater fullness of life. Let them be read slowly and reflectively.

"Do not be afraid. Listen, I bring you news of a great joy, a joy to be shared by the whole people." (Luke 2:10)

"I have told you this
so that my joy may be in you
and your joy be complete." (John 15:11)

"Every time I pray for all of you, I pray with joy." (Philippians 1:3)

- Inner happiness and even quiet joy are possible for those who spend time with the Lord. Are we able to discover the source of our joy in a personal or a community encounter with Jesus? Are we able to provide sufficient time for such moments?
- Sharing the joy of the Gospel is what the consecrated life is all about; "no one is excluded by the joy brought by the Lord" (Paul VI, *Gaudete in Domino*, 22). How can we as religious bring hope and joy to those on the margins?

Meditation and reflection

"There are Christians whose lives seem like Lent without Easter" (*Evangelii Gaudium*, 6). It is true that we can spend six weeks in penitential practices during Lent; rarely, however, do religious communities spend the six weeks after Easter in joyful celebration. Can we change this mind-set?

- "By his coming Christ has brought eternal newness. With this newness he is always able to renew our lives and our communities" (*Evangelii Gaudium*, 1). Inner renewal is our goal in this Year of the Consecrated Life. This in turn will bring community renewal and newness. Reflect on this possibility.
- Counterfeit joy is often a danger for religious people. Authentic joy comes from personal relationships. How is it possible to revive this "renewed personal encounter with Jesus Christ" that Pope Francis refers to in his *Exhortation*?

Prayer and supplication

"But now I am coming to you,
and while still in the world I say these things
to share my joy within them to the full." (John 17:13)

- Praying for the gift of happiness or joy may appear to be selfish and not in our tradition. However, it is a Gospel precept: "Until now you have not asked for anything in my name. Ask and you will receive, and so your joy will be complete." (John 16:24)
- Karl Jung, the father of modern psychology, used to say that the majority of the population leads quiet lives of bland despair... lives without a spark. Perhaps some members of our communities also feel isolated, anxious or marginalised. We pray that a spark of God's love may enliven those in difficulty.

Sharing vision and resolutions

Perhaps we can use three of the questions Pope Francis asks to expand our vision and help us make resolutions. (See *Rejoice*, paragraphs 44-45)

- "I want to say one word to you and this word is 'joy'. Whenever there are consecrated people, seminarians, men and women religious, young people, there is always joy! It is the joy of following Jesus." Are we part of this joy?
- "Looking into the depth of your heart …has your heart preserved the restlessness of seeking, or have you let it be suffocated by things that end by hardening it? God awaits you, he seeks you; how do you respond to him?"
- "We are victims of the temporary… How can I be free, how can I break free from this 'culture of the temporary'?" In other words, Pope Francis invites us to liberation and true joy.

Preparation for the next meeting

Arrange the date and the time for the next meeting, and invite a member of the community to coordinate it and prepare the final celebration.

Celebration

To conclude, recall those you have lived with who were a source of joy to you and to others. Then have a real celebration, sharing food, drink and conversation, remembering them with affection.

Session Nine
She who Walks with Us

Theme: Mary, companion on our journey.
Aspects: Mother of the Church; model disciple; pilgrim.

Texts for orientation

"Do whatever he tells you." (John 2:5)

"There is a Marian 'style' to the Church's work of evangelization. Whenever we look to Mary, we come to believe once again in the revolutionary nature of love and tenderness. In her we see that humility and tenderness are not virtues of the weak but of the strong who need not treat others poorly in order to feel important themselves." (*Evangelii Gaudium*, 288)

"Virgin of the Visitation, we entrust them (consecrated persons) that they may go forth to meet human needs, to being help, but above all to bring Jesus. Teach then to proclaim the mighty things God accomplishes in the world that all peoples may extol the greatness of his name. Support them in their work for the poor, the hungry, those without hope, the little ones and all who seek your Son with a sincere heart." (*Vita Consecrata*, 112)

Introduction

On the table place an icon of Mary, the mother of Jesus. A candle is lit, and some traditional prayers to the Blessed Mother, such as the *Hail Holy Queen* or the *Memorare* are recited.

Lived Experience

- Since the earliest days of religious and community life, Mary has been seen as our patroness and companion.
- In your life as a religious, what has Mary meant for you?
- What place does she have in your community?
- Mary has a privileged place as Mother of the Church. Her physical and spiritual proximity to Jesus place her close to the mystery of redemption. How is your missionary role in the Church lived out in the spirit of Mary?

The Word of God

Let us now read the text of John 2:1-5.
The reading should be done slowly, clearly and with a period of silence.

Three days later there was a wedding at Cana in Galilee. The mother of Jesus was there, and Jesus and his disciples had also been invited. When they ran out of wine, since the wine provided for the wedding was all finished, the mother of Jesus said to him, "They have no wine". Jesus said, "Woman, why turn to me? My hour has not come yet."

- How do you understand the words of Mary in this passage?
- How do they apply to us?

Meditation and reflection

Mary gathered with the fragile and fearful community in prayer, as they waited for the Spirit at Pentecost. Reflect on the place Mary has in your life and your community today. The *Rosary* for example is a time-honoured means of reflection, although it can be difficult for some to pray publically. Are we able to pray even one decade in a meditative manner?

Pray to Mary quietly, or use a vocal prayer such as the **Memorare** *or the* **Hail Mary.**

Prayer and supplication

In the spirit of this meditation, the community now prays Mary's *Magnificat* (Luke 1:46-55).

And Mary said:
"My soul proclaims the greatness of the Lord
and my spirit exults in God my saviour;
because he has looked upon his lowly handmaid.
Yes, from this day forward all generations will call me blessed,
for the Almighty has done great things for me.
Holy is his name,
and his mercy reaches from age to age for those who fear him.
He has shown the power of his arm,
he has routed the proud of heart.
He has pulled down princes from their thrones
    and exalted the lowly.
The hungry he has filled with good things,
    the rich sent empty away.
He has come to the help of Israel his servant,
    mindful of his mercy
    – according to the promise he made to our ancestors –
    of his mercy to Abraham and to his descendants for ever."

We are invited to choose a verse which reflects our own journey, and then pray it in our own words.

- How do I glorify God?
- Do I allow God to fill my emptiness?
- Recall the marvels the Lord has done for you and for your Order or Congregation.

Sharing vision and resolutions

What initiatives can I as an individual and we as a community take to rekindle and deepen our devotion to Mary?

- How might our particular community's devotion to the mother of Jesus enliven and encourage the proclamation of the Word of God throughout the country and the world?
- Public novenas and well-arranged services in honour of Mary, open to the public, can be a source of help and consolation to many in need. Can we offer or be involved in any of these?

Preparation for the next meeting

Arrange the date and the time for the next meeting, and invite a member of the community to coordinate it and prepare the final celebration.

Celebration

To conclude, have a community celebration in honour of our Blessed Lady in the community room, and then some snacks and drinks afterwards.

Face to Face – the Final Encounter

Theme: Fidelity and the encounter with God.

Aspects: The covenant of love; faithfulness; the final journey.

Texts for orientation

"Now we are seeing a dim reflection in a mirror; but then we shall be seeing face to face."
(1 Corinthians 13:12)

"I know who it is that I have put my trust in." (2 Timothy 1:12)

"What will take place on the other side when all for me will be overturned into eternity, I do not know. I believe, I truly believe only that a great love awaits me."
(St John of the Cross)

"For when Christ shall appear and the glorious resurrection of the dead takes place, the splendour of God will brighten the heavenly city and the Lamb will be the lamp. Then in the supreme happiness of charity the whole Church of the saints will adore God and the 'Lamb who was slain', proclaiming with one voice: 'To him who sits upon the throne, and to the Lamb, blessing and honour and glory and dominion, for ever and ever' (Apocalypse 5:13-14)." (*Perfectae Caritatis*, 51)

Introduction

On a table place a crucifix, an icon of Our Lady and a symbol of the Easter tomb. A candle is lit, and some photos of community members who have died and gone before us are placed on the table in gratitude and love.

Lived Experience

Fidelity is a personal challenge and an invitation from Jesus.

- What helps have you used, and what helps do you need, to remain faithful?
- In the journey through religious life how does, and how can, the community assist us?
- How can we support, in a very real way, those who are seriously ill? How can we support our older members as they prepare for the final journey to eternity?

The Word of God

Let us now read the text of 1 Thessalonians 4:13-18.
The reading should be done slowly, clearly and with a period of silence.

We want to be quite certain, brothers, about those who have died, to make sure that you do not grieve about them, like the other people who have no hope. We believe that Jesus died and rose again, and that it will be the same for those who have died in Jesus: God will bring them with him. We can tell you this from the Lord's own teaching, that any of us who are left alive until the Lord's coming will not have any advantage over those who have died. At the trumpet of God, the voice of the archangel will call out the command and the Lord himself will come down from heaven; those who have died in Christ will be the first to rise, and then those of us who are still alive will be taken up in the clouds, together with them, to meet the Lord in the air. So we shall stay with the Lord for ever. With such thoughts as these you should comfort one another.

- How do you feel about the last moments of life?
- What are your fears and your hopes about death?

Meditation and reflection

We belong to God and to the Church. The people of God have a right to our fidelity. "The consecrated life is important precisely in its being unbounded generosity and love." (*Vita Consecrata*, 105)

"Do not forget the charisms which have shaped remarkable 'seekers of God' and benefactors of humanity, who have provided sure paths for those seeking God with a sincere heart." (*Vita Consecrata*, 109)

- How can I be more faithful in the ordinary and small things of life?
- How can we, as a community, be more faithful, and how can we be witnesses as a joyful community, living in expectation of the encounter with God?

Prayer and supplication

"All shall be well. And all shall be well. And all manner of things shall be well." (Julian of Norwich)

- In surrender and trust let us pray quietly, "Into your hands, Lord, I commend my spirit."
- Let us spend some time holding before God those in our religious orders and congregations who have gone before us, and on whose dedication our communities have been built and sustained.

Sharing vision and resolutions

- What practical steps can we take to make more real, the concept of a watchful, hopeful and joyful community as described by Pope Francis?
- Is there any more we can do for our elderly, sick or dying members? What further spiritual assistance can we offer them?
- Honouring those who have gone to God is part of our heritage. How shall we continue to do this? How may we make this more meaningful?

Celebration

To conclude, have a community celebration in honour of our beloved dead. Have some pictures and photographs of our deceased members on the table and make them a real part of the celebration – with some snacks and drinks to honour them.